SERPENT'S TOOTH

POEMS

STERLING WARNER

Sterling Warner

Serpent's Tooth: Poems
Copyright © by Sterling Warner 2021
All Rights Reserved

This book may not be reproduced in whole or part, in
any form (beyond that permitted by Sections 107 and 108
of the U. S. Copyright Law and except by reviewers
for the purpose of criticism and review), without
written permission of the publisher.

Published in the United States of America
First Printing: 2021

ISBN: 9798703447352
Independent Publishers, Inc

Cover Layout: Sterling Warner
Cover Photo: *Cobra.* Public Domain

Multifaceted, a jewel of a book set in carved out sections. Observant verse, a multiverse: part past, past potential — lines cast in Freedom's river, twice. This is a poetry that bites deep. Sharp as a Serpent's Tooth.
—**Lorna Dee Cervantes:** Poet, Author of *Sueño: New Poems* and *Emplumada*

Whether contemplating nature, calling out social inequities, or excavating complicated memories, in *Serpent's Tooth* Sterling Warner's love for the English language is on display. Chameleon-like, he seems comfortable with almost any subject, in almost any poetic form. This new collection is a treasure trove of tonal variety, wit, and rumination. As the old maps used to say about uncharted territories, here be dragons!
—**David Denny,** author of *Some Divine Commotion* and *Fool in the Attic*

An engaging storyteller, Sterling Warner takes us on a magic carpet ride with King Lear and Ella Fitzgerald through memory, hope, and emotion. Whether reflecting on Covid-19 or smokes behind the house, observing a sunrise or rapid transit traffic, Warner is a wordsmith whose love of language sparks whatever he touches.
—**Chella Courington:** Writer, Educator, Author of *Adele and Tom: The Portrait of a Marriage* and *In Their Own Way*

Sterling's poems witness texture and digging into memory and imagination, something for everyone: to make us laugh and cry and ponder—a voice that loves sound, meaning, and wordplay. His poems vibrate off the page as expressions and discovery: dense and airy, fluid and structured…tender, vital, vivacious verse.
—**Tobey Kaplan:** Poet, Educator, Author of *Across the Great Divide: Selected Poems*

An inspiring collection of poetry: some light-hearted and others deeply personal, giving insight into the poet's vast array of experiences and the meaning of life.
—**Birdman313:** Poet, Author of *Words from the Heart* and *Poetry in the Wind*

Sterling Warner's sixth volume of poetry, *Serpent's Tooth,* invites the reader into an energetic universe where King Lear, Gilgamesh, Ēostre, Apollo and Bob Dylan rub shoulders with fireflies, the ever-present albatross, skunks and the poet's grandma, all populating a place where the past is as alive as the future and every corner of every hick town is as gloriously alluring as Notre Dame Cathedral. Everyone is welcome here—in sorrow, loss, and exuberant joy, you will be glad you entered Warner's world of "Words, Words, Words."
—**Rose Anna Higashi:** English Professor, Poet, Blogger, author of *Finding the Poet* (mybestpoetry.com), *Blue Wings* and "Tea and Travels" (myteaplanner.com)

This is a wide-ranging and generous book of gifts. Warner is a talented storyteller full of wonder, wisdom, praise, and love.
—**Lee Herrick:** Poet, Educator, Author of *Scar and Flower and Gardening Secrets of the Dead*

Serpent's Tooth: Poems is a soul stirring volume of eclectic poetry. It has something for everyone - whether it takes one down memory lane in "Aide Memoire," praises humanity in "Acclamations," expresses sorrow for the dear departed in "Treasured," or captures a precious carpe diem moment in "Kodak." The vividly electric verse enhances the readers' imagination and resonates with them at all levels.
—**Roohi Vora:** Medical Doctor, English Professor, Director SJAWP and contributor to various literary magazines

Sterling Warner's poetry spans a lifetime of consideration and adoration for the human language, whether it is in response to nature's fickleness, the passage of time, or society's endless follies. *Serpent's Tooth* is a literary collage of Warner's aptitude for turning the mundanity of the everyday into masterful observations of life's wonders and fragilities. As alliteration dances between lines and poetic forms, when spoken out loud the poems in *Serpent's Tooth* reveal the glee, snark, and subtle humor of a man who weighs his words against a future yet written.
—**Danny "Dandiggity" Le**: Poet, Librarian, Community Liaison, Creative Consultant

Poetry to be reckoned with. Sterling has powerful love of rubbing words together. Follow the lion and the dragon dancer, consider "intriguing antiquity", and finish with frank reflections on COVID-19.
—**NanLeah Mick:** A self-taught naturalist, poet, photographer and poetographerm

SERPENT'S TOOTH: POEMS

PAPER MOONS

Lion and Dragon Dancers

Chinese
New Year,
Traditional
Celebration,
Lion dancers blink eyes
As large as beach balls
Expose furry jaws,
Accept Red Envelopes and
Various other gifts,
Make way for the Dragon
Dancers—a dozen plus
Legs shaking
Lung's yellow
Bold back arching
Acrobatic arms raising
Majestically
Lifting a torso on poles;
Dragon head's
Animated cranium nodding,
Mouth opening,
Speaking in cryptic voices
While skilled acrobats
Twist and turn its long
Segmented, serpentine body,

Adorned in spark throwing fireworks,
    Tail keeping time to strong,
        Steady drum beats,
           Encircling the pillar with
                Angular, rhythmic movements,
            Cavorting, Gamboling, Capering
        Mixing *Cloud Cave, Whirlpool,* and
      Threading the Money dance patterns,
Projecting dignity, fertility, and power,

Leaving me a spectator rather than a
    Participant as my sweetheart teases
        The dragon seeking wisdom by
           Chasing a pearl—symbolic
           Ball on a stick—
              Zig-zagging
                Out of emotion,
             Out of reach,
         Out of love,
      Out of luck.

Loveland: A Sestina
For Jen and John

Early morning Eastern mist and Rocky Mountains
Moisture evaporated as increasing sunrays
Fingered their way across the still sleepy valley,
Urging daylight sounds to thrive, mingle, and wander:
Fresh, fecund, flowers opening, fragrances traveling,
All summer signs seemed perfect for a June wedding.

Lightly packed suitcase guests arrived at Jen's wedding.
Some star sleepers planned to pitch tents on the mountains.
Expecting to camp and fish after tense traveling
East and west to celebrate amid warm sunrays.
Secretly seeking a mile high then to wander
Dusty western sites haunted ghost towns down valley.

Airport delays, grave foreboding in the valley,
Though people worried heat waves might spoil Jen's wedding,
Dark clouds approached near and far then didn't wander,
Rooted to the Rockies, dropping snow on Mountains,
Blanketing earth and campers like icy sunrays,
Bodies presuming mosquitoes'd vex their traveling.

Climatologists forecast tips while traveling—
Patterns unpredictable in Loveland Valley.
Hoping sporadic drizzle'd give way to sunrays,
Fearing naught, all plans proceeded for Jen's wedding;
Even snowcapped peaks on cool, majestic Mountains
Seemed to melt, while clouds like Wordsworth rose to wander.

Some skewered hors d'oeuvres, so did not rest or wander
Before rites began—dances sent them traveling
Back to the airport or highway through the mountains,
Journey's with brief advisories through the valley;
Minds urged on a calm for the late afternoon wedding,
Undaunted by Sols' lackluster spray of sunrays.

Bridal and groom parties posed in shades sans sunrays,
Inclement skies caused no cameras to wander
Away; the procession, vows, toasts at Jen's wedding
Remained front and center, ere guests commenced traveling;
Music resounded like a rich, boombox valley,
Rhythmic dancing feet echoed off granite mountains.

Guests who spread like sunrays began their traveling,
Ceasing to fret and wander around Loveland's Valley,
Down the air-light mountains, following Jen's wedding.

Treasured
(For Debbie: R.I.P.)

Fist
dirt
filled, tossed
on a brass & oak
coffin, tears mingled
with early morning mist,
walking from the cemetery,
my sister's final resting place.

Debbie's memory hangs
before my face like
turquoise earrings
pulling down
lobes, getting
heavier as
years
pass.

Aide-Mémoire

Every wrinkle tells a tale,
each crease a reminder of
painful and pleasurable pacts,
dues paid fortune's piper;
present laugh lines become
future furrows that mark
quizzical moments speculating,
waiting like a footman for
silent answers; furtive glances
into mirrors overlook contours,
scars, liver spots, blemishes
when shriveled mouths mimic
youthful lips forming words,
elicit unexceptional memories
of people, places, and things
best forgotten, rationalize
unkept promises as bad timing,
bringing them firmly into focus
where good news and ill tidings
exact an equal price for experience:
enduring folds freely offered in
exchange for eventual anecdotes.

Kodak

Mom and babe on a grassy knoll
picnicking on the
park's grass, same
turf folks
walk
dogs,
teens
toss
Frisbees,
parents watch
children play & scream,
seniors mull over their faint past;
photographer dad directs his
camera's best shot.
aperture,
sharpens
the
view;
babe
and
mom coached,
"Please smile now."
"Click!" A time capsule's
captured, candidly unaltered.

Blizzard Bling

Remembering Washington State's Snowmageddon: 2019

Flurries fall on asphalt, brick, and gravel roads
covering coal black soot, masking filth, grime, and dirt
transforming solid waste and refuse into an
ornamental winter wonderland, unsullied and chaste.

Lifeless lawns convert into blanched, crunchy carpets
invasive Himalayan blackberry vines become
linked jewel laurels, glistening from highways as
they climb unimpeded 'till they crown mountain peaks.

Like snowplows, cars push fiercely forward over
suburban streets and cluttered freeways, their puttering gait
reminding drivers nature alone controls the weather while humans
thwart organic solutions to catastrophes affecting climate change.

Naked, deciduous trees alongside evergreen cedar, pine, and redwood
branches bend bows, carefully cradling wintery loads seemingly
proud to shoulder icy burdens increase in size and weight—flake
upon flake—across slender, sizeable cellulose arms indiscriminately.

Unlike rhythmic raindrop pounding—pelting—people, places, things
snow silently sneaks up on all living creatures, floating through the
atmosphere like magical, minute, silver frost moths—delicate ice angels
that lay mutely on objects or thaw inaudibly after falling.

Taffeta Turnover Fibonacci

(or Wednesday's Half Price)

All
eyes
on the
countertop,
Salvation Army
merchandise: slick wicker woven
Easter baskets with artificial grass 50 years—
a half century ago; moths settle on sallow, antique lampshades, calf skin tightly
wrapped around the bells, askew, atop tarnished brass poles
rightly placed in creepy corners;
carved baroque bookshelves,
cast off by
Gen-X
lads
lost
in
their
witless
love affair
with plumb ugliness;
music box ballerinas turn
deftly, pirouetting *en pointe*, crackled salt shakers,
plastic boots, silk brassieres an array of colors & sizes; where else might evidence
lockers unload perfectly good clothes, bath towels, shoes,
or forensic file cabinets
filled with cold cases?
Second hand
goods seem
first
class.

Arachne's Star

Birds begin to sing only minutes before
dawn's bright smile lights up early morning,
creating prisms as sunrays pass through
dewdrops caught on spiderwebs & bats fly into
    dark awnings, accessible attics, & open barns.

Chirping seems to simultaneously cease as
if a conductor clued-in all feathered friends
the appropriate time to feed on worms that
gather in garden dirt and uncut lawns,
    to enjoy a brief respite from saturated soil.

From daybreak unbound until midnight's edge,
nature's rituals continue, creatures consummate
circadian habits & adventurous moments as
the master weaving spider, Arachne, extends
    artistic masterpieces, persevering 'til tomorrow.

Spontaneity: Chasing Crazy

Dancing the tango down main street
      grabbing complete stranger's hands
leading partners chest-to-chest, alternating
      upper thigh & hips proactively, like a sailor
on leave, steppin' out, swaying like Dean Martin
      taking small steps *three sheets to the wind.*

Skipping smooth, flat stones across shallow koi ponds,
      ripples roll like miniature arching waves
crashing into rooted water plants along the shoreline;
      sitting for hours at railway junctions watching trains
waiting for the streamlined Denver Zephyr, observing only
      two level louvered stock cars transporting pigs & cattle.

Gamboling though downpours without umbrella,
      kicking colorful oil rings resting on puddles,
ducking inside an all-night FM radio station
      at the edge of town, announcing call letters before
introducing an uninterrupted hour of Pink Floyd classics
      returning to deserted sidewalks, owning them till dawn.

Intersections

Our cubist love life seemed like
a quaint collage of sharp angles,
clever left-handed compliments,
right brain assumptions that

merged in severe cerebral cortex
corners, fed our interminable
sexual appetites formerly satisfied by
duel posturing, youthful swagger;

incline planes linked, we knit brows
then fashioned a coefficient future together
always with mathematical precision—
naïve thoughts indifferent to accuracy;

outdoors we persisted, daily attitude
adjustments seemed spirited by insincerity,
yet amorous beach lounge antics morphed
into degrees of compassion, transcending

our gradient relationship, recapturing exploited
emotions—squandered opportunities—as rainclouds
harassed us with dire, protractor earnest; creatures
of habit, eyes half-shut, we slept on edges in rooms

where burnt sienna ceilings met beige plaster walls,
mirrors hung everywhere like a carousel sanctuary;
calculating fractal dimensions, our abstract affair
connected avant-garde aesthetics via geometric forms;

meticulously measuring & critiquing each other's
opinions, polite, punctilious ministers of decorum—
we celebrated harmony, yet honored all differences
as gravely as free-floating Green Lake lanterns.

CAVALCADES

Hood Canal Sunrise

Aurora washes sleep from the
horizon's firmly shut eyes, pushes
thick morning mist apart like
velvet, tear soaked, theatre curtains,
allows the moisture to trickle down
her dawning naked body—a multicolored
palette—that passionately paints a creeping
radiance, creates rainbow virgin visas,
pure, unsullied, provocative, unrepentant;
as dewdrops drip off plant petals,
sunshine grazes grass blades leaving
liquid trails of melody & mirth,
she strokes her mother's chilly cheeks
at sunrise with rosy fingered aplomb
while Sol's bold beams send
feverish warmth through loose soil
like earthworms penetrating sandy
silt or decayed organic matter,
making steamy vapors float skyward
like evaporating helium lifting
chimaera dreamscapes aloft,
until twilight shades the visual
spectacle and twinkling stars guide
Aurora to Oceanus' edge, time spent
mixing daybreak pigments for tomorrow.

Giselle & Albrecht Reborn

Liberated from lockdowns, self-doubt's
shackles, caution's curiosity, psychic's
premonitions, & certainty's restrictions,
we crawled through pussy willows on
our bellies, indirectly snaking our way
in serpentine fashion to the Bolshoi river.

Damp, nitrogen-rich soil smelled of
decomposing vegetation, a holy fragrance
that permeated the enchanted embankment
like invisible, ghostly incense—yet stimulated
our soft muscles, once puffy as under-eye bags,
precipitously taunt, firm, toned, pumped, primed.

Nature transformed my love into a prima ballerina
in street clothes & PF Flyers— Margot Fonteyn
to my flamboyant Rudolf Nureyev maneuvers—
after I spread my legs, began to jump, performed
double tours, cabrioles, & attitude turns, she
effortlessly countered with picturesque pirouettes.

Along the waterfront, our two free souls defied gravity
& gravitas alike, no longer searching for a quayside,
we just relished the woodland Royal Ballet; uplifted by
auspicious, enigmatic dance steps, an impromptu
tour de force—light, airy, elegant, & buoyant—we
froze time's trepidation amid moments of endless levity.

Intrepid Belle

a
lone
ashen
cigarette
hangs like a minute
smoldering lamppost held between
flawless charcoal lips perpetually pouting; puffing
drag after drag, saintly halos
circle her raven
hair with
smoky
grey
crowns

eyes
gaze
beyond
vague New Year's
resolutions, she
earmarks pageantry for future
emancipations; crossed arms convey sheer attitude,
glares caution each discomforting
conviction—yet brows
visibly
invite
love's
touch

Acclamations

Praise to all first responders, medical workers,
firefighters, peace officers & volunteer staff
      Women & men who lay down their
      lives in the service of strangers.

Praise to all drummers who
swagger rhythmically out to battle
      to the ones who lay down beats for
      marching band and color guard footsteps.

Praise to affectionate, lofty lovers
who lie down indifferent to turbulence,
      making time for themselves immersed
      in the moment and a future less bleak.

Kudos to all the single mothers, orphans and
civil servants dedicated to common sense,
      whose passion's most perfect and ideals
      unquestioned when seeking preservation.

Hats off to our entertainers who
amuse even as our assaulted minds moan
      and remind us there's more to life than
      soundbites showcasing disasters, and defeat.

Praise to the dilettantes, poets, pipers,
philosophers, and politicians, without whom
      we'd have no visionaries, revolutionaries, leaders, or
      blind tyrants casting evil apparitions to oppress us.

Praise to the workers, vacationers and the
indolent for roads traveled often without reward—
      experiences and achievements compressed into memorable
      moments, while pressured to exceed high expectations.

Praise to the multitude, society's unwashed faces,
sporting smiling mouths full of partial teeth, conveying
      generosity, goodness and sensitivity, seldomly
      measured accurately by acumen or wealth.

Evergreen

boughs
hang
apple
heavy as
silhouette Christians
adopt traditions align the
nativity with winter's solstice, adorn tables
with yuletide camellias, Christmas
haggis, teaming neeps,
tatties, toast
auld lang
syne
days

Onus

Coerced by delirious desire, piercing ice packed peaks of
mountains ravaged by a blizzard's furious bombardment,

induced by a firestorm of perfect passion where purpose plays me
like a violin, draws its bow across my body tuned in perfect fifths,

obliged as any apostle to spread the saintly word of love's
spiritual transcendence intermingled with physical lust,

compelled by beauty's wintery commitment to smoother
naked promises with kisses, avert dissembling romance,

required to honor amour, traverse submission's maze, trace
devotion's future footsteps through snow tracks from the past.

Shadow Spiral

Spinning down memories
like an antique centrifuge
separating bile from bright moments
friendships from convenient companions,
the pharmacy philosopher recites the
Hippocratic oath, crosses his body,
prescribes himself a modicum of memoirs,
a dose of nostalgia, a gram of regret.

Distorting blithe romances
recalling better amorous outcomes
placing fantasy before actual engagements
conquests before mutual satisfaction;
he drifts upon a sophist's cloud,
dominates all intellectual conversations,
displays skill and stamina in argumentation,
ignores ethos and logos in the art of persuasion.

Exploring scrappy remembrances becomes
an epic ordeal—a dead-end scavenger hunt where
both deceptive and reliable *silhouettes* shade
the would-be physician's self-image;
sorting out perfect pledges from broken promises
sets his perpetual wheel of dissonance turning,
picks up momentum with each revolution,
isolates unfiltered thoughts like solids and liquids.

Call Me Easter

The Lady of the Lake's hands buoyed me, a
floundering drake atop glassy waters, 'til gifting
my panic to a denim blue farm boy on shore who
cradled my belly between his elbow & forearm

my downy body compressed like a pillow
against the teen, left me gasping for air,
seeking reprieve in the sinful lagoon where
tears pool into the tarn—nature's baptismal font

thrashing like a clueless saffron-faced POTUS or
prime minister, my ebon eyes glanced through vagabond
strands of a straw-yellow hairpiece, gazing afar at
feathered flocks—freedom on wing flying north

as if in mourning, I watched my present glide into the past;
restrictive movement prevented me from joining either
through actions or memories, doomed to recall
intermittent, quixotic quacking as the Lake Lady's perfect

palms & slender sylph-like fingers rescued all that's
dysfunctional, delivering me from nothing but my
pathetic fowl fortune: an inability to lead ducklings,
inspire followers—let alone fatten-up for dinner.

Grandma's Kitchen

On first entering the Willow Glen house,
I passed below Spanish archways, adobe walls,
& smiled at the comforting smell of old people
not realizing the welcoming aroma's a mixture of
sweat, Lord Calvert, Kool cigarettes & cigar smoke.

Grandma's kitchen changed that pungent dynamic
beginning at 4 PM when she began to brown
whatever meat she would cook for our supper; her
cast-iron frying pan sputtered grease everywhere
but, on task, she seldom stopped to wipe up or clean.

Fortified by heavy clip-earrings (my trademark cheap gift),
Grandma always wore a hand sown cotton apron over the
same white polka dot blue dress like a culinary uniform
tied in a perfect bow that rested atop her corpulent rump
like a Siamese cast sprawled out on freshly washed towels

Wedged in ceramic jars, wooden spoons stood at attention,
ready to mix her secret recipes, stir the magic ingredients;
a kitchen wall exhaust fan pulled aromatic scents through
the circular porthole—fragrances emanating from her oven,
into night's pitch—crafted by her spotted, wizened hands.

Grandma saved me in college from subsisting on tuna fish;
when I visited, she'd prepared me an entire leg of lamb; slicing
into its flesh, making X marks, sliding slim slivers of garlic,
cloves, & onions inside; I'd leave with all leftovers (nostrils still
inhaling mint jelly) & an earnest invitation to visit more often.

Virginia Valediction Revisited: A Haibun
For David, My Brother

Tanbark trails stretch out like splintered, spiritual highways from DC/Dulles airfields to Virginian hills where ticks pepper arms and legs, digging in for corkscrew supper. These days seek measurement—refinement—amid structural chaos, a cosmos aligned through promise, scientific certainty seeking emotional purgation. The feral child within us all grasps for clues to clarify craft and lore, honoring heritage, suckling life span's variations.

Gazing across glassy chocolate colored waters, a pond where baritone bullfrogs set nature's metronome in motion. Buzzing June-bugs quicken the pace: clicking...clicking ...clicking..., and the woods, the trees, the eastern seaboard's song cradle cries from lonesome memories healthy heartaches, anniversaries that might have been, yet remain empty fountains, fragile unexplored possibilities.

Championing ecology, resting on religion, David quivered like an arrow through wind gusts, arching, piercing an emerald Charlottesville meadow. Exodus followed triumphant smiles, tortured tears, truncated, courageous fellowships, as his life's ripple splashed outwards, curled like circular embraces, moved every direction, clutched for land, merged with twilight's chorus, *adagio*, became one with the lofty landscape, till pastoral harmonies softly faded, leaving behind still water's wake.

motley colored leaves,
nature's tattoos, awaken
memories past

CANVAS SKIES

Danaë's Perseid

Hail, hail, hail; let me lie beneath
Zeus's majestic, ancient canopy,
dwell in imagination's pageantry
where I, like Danaë, behold showers of
gold, when ebon skies discharge
blazing meteors bombarding
earth from an apparent radiant,
heavens celestial point,
the constellation of Perseus.

The Perseids cloud stretches
like a bling covered house cat
stride for stride pacing the
Swift Tuttle comet, its orbit
empowered by nubile
dust mixing with debris,
forming a volatile, shimmering,
glittering mass—shooting stars
piercing the firmament.

Predawn fireflies linger too briefly;
their rising tails, crossettes and dahlias,
dance across the blushing northern
welkin, a transitory aerial spectacle
whose strobing peonies and Saturn shells
dwindle into flickering bottle rockets,
become mere sparks against emerging dawn;
awe struck still, my night sky memories
immortalize fair Danaë's annual golden rainfall.

Gretta's Mirror

Brown eyes glare, fixate on walls
gaining renewed appreciation for
communal cobwebs & scientific
certainty of social justice between
eight legged architects, sticky silk arachnid
nets, now hosting mere exoskeletons.

From spiderweb construction sites,
Gretta glances though bay view
windows, noticing squirrels race
around her front porch & mud
swallows build nets under eves,
nature unhindered by quarantines.

Gretta's black pearl choker highlights
her long neck, not kissed by outsiders
since lockdown began; long bangs now
cropped & shaved, shaped like postage
stamps; her thick, coarse bun emerging
from a smooth, shadowy, feminine skull.

Stark reflections today belie pure beauty
tomorrow; with or without the benefit of
artifice, she'll mingle among the masses
mouth showing teeth, laughter replacing
pensive pondering, accepting a new normal,
anxiously waiting on Amazon to deliver earrings.

Lincoln Green

Robin Hood Restaurant
A long way from Sherwood Forest,
Nottingham nonsense, the crusading
Norman: King Richard who spent but
Three years in British Isles....
The same hand-hewn benches, tables
Cross nature's paths, appearing like
Stacked linking logs from walnut tree
Highways interlinked overhead.

Cool water briskly splashes against
Twigs, pebbles and palm sized rocks as
Minnows navigate mini sandstone and
Granite boulders like elegant ballet dancers
Shifting, turning, alighting on toe, some
Breaking the swift stream to capture
Flecks of floating food or flying insects:
Nature's system of checks and balances
broadly displayed sans King John power grab.

Open pits filled with hickory and oak
Outdoors, beef and lamb roast on spits
Gridirons cook first and bar-be-cue pork
skewered flesh spits, hot juices merge, and
Prime rib rolls off bones, melts into mouths
While flagons of ale mix laughter and mirth
Moving a medieval merrymaking setting into
An imaginary war weary world now
Firmly re-rooted in a real-time fantasy.

Under Rainbows

Alacrity opened my
eyes before dawn
as birds fluffed dust
off night wing feathers
started chirping as shadowy
skies shed light.

Deep, restful sleep
fortified my weary mind
gave me strength to
question relationship obstacles
heal my wasteland of dreams
with a 21st century grail.

Last night, courtesy beckoned,
modesty responded, Judice
listened; my terse words of affection
caught her caution off guard
yet I missed a genuine chance
to bond beyond curt amorous clichés.

As sun rays peaked over
the Olympia Mountain range
alone, the bird choir softens
its saccharine song
past poor decisions strengthen
my present, positive resolve.

Grinding Fibonacci

Like
line
dancers
bumping and
grinding, bodies brush
each other intentionally
touch denim—cause for banter apologies, pick-up
lines and cocktail absolution—
chess move prelude where
knight takes queen,
walks out
the
door
booze
numb,
no plans
to sober up
'til more drinks
consummate magical late night
madness with midnight's flickering street lamp dignity,
early morning disbeliefs stripped
of surprises, air
sedating
senses
come
dawn.

Hamartia Unbound

Cassiopeia glares down at me
    from the heavens
        chained to a tortuous chair, reflecting
            on her vanity
        forlorn, constantly fanning herself
            with a palm leaf,
        longing to behold her beauteous face
            in a pearl-handle mirror.

Cassiopeia now showers night skies
    with her silvery studded constellation
        wheeling her throne like a stellar convalescent
            about the Celestial North pole
        spending half her time circling the globe
            upside-down, sending blood to her head
        the "earth- shaker's" fitting punishment
            for disparaging sea nymphs.

Cepheus sits by Cassiopeia's side brooding
    as undeserving among planets as humans,
        guilty of offering Andromeda to Cetus,
            atonement for the Queen Mother's crimes;
        (what's with comparing mother daughter beauty
            to goddesses, Nereids, female water spirits?)
        Husband and wife filicide co-conspirators' fate
            merits Medusa's gaze—not a star eternity.

Ode to a Harvest Fly

Cicada minstrel sings for me,
vibrates membranes,
creates sounds
that amplify, resonate
from branch to branch,
leaf to leaf, tree to tree,
their high-pitched drone,
a passionate, piercing buzz,
fills the quiet hush of shadowy
forest floors—summer's silent,
corners—lightens up
my somber, pensive thoughts,
ushers on courageous,
life affirming wails,
permeating daylight hours
with July's concerto,
August's symphony,
Mother Nature's
circadian melodies.

Kerchief Nostalgia

Inhaling fresh hope, exhaling dysfunction
justice on edge enjoys an extended hiatus as
concealed compassion sighs then gasps,
bleeds through sepia photograph frames (respire)
—*breathe* truths unshakable, unique, enduring
like unalterable antique daguerreotype
images—distorted only by demigods in the
guise of deliverance, panting false prophets
offering quixotic sermons. caverns of choice,
elliptical dreams, progressive barriers of oblivion.

Saltine crackers linked with kite string form
a makeshift sleep mask, attempt to shield
honest eyes cringing at impending disasters,
like unfulfilled promises of safety and accountability,
convincingly uttered during Grenfell Tower Fire aftermath,
where equity's been obscured by political discourse,
envy and covetousness defined civilized parameters,
perpetually privileging a select few. *Keep breathing;*
let lasting change rise from the phoenix's ashes,
may the glue binding all to a revolution resist factions.

Of Lionels & Red Barons

Steam trains & biplanes vicariously
moving travelers point to point
panting locomotives passionately
pull passenger cars, sparks flying,
jolting bodies along hard ribbons of steel tracks,
rack & pinon wheels grinding on adhesion railways,
thunder rolling en route to Texaco stations
while wannabe Manfred von Richthofens
maneuver top heavy bi-planes high above,
errant eyes beneath goggles fixate on mischief;
bored, the pilots toss *Coca-Cola* bottles into
coal beds below ala *The Gods Must be Crazy,*
followed by additional cockpit trash aimed
at the scarlet caboose, any bombardier's delight.

FREEFALL

Intriguing Antiquity

My niece introduced me to friends
as an *intriguing antiquity,* someone
brought into the world long before
cell phones, twitter, texts, and rap;
her comrades bumped my elbow
with senior diffidence; they urged
me share memorable moments

before I'd been born, navigating hardships
during the 1929 stock market crash & kissing
girls in Times Square following WWII.

"My uncle's still an antique," my niece
proudly assured. "He's a baby-boomer—
well over half a century old!" I nodded
winked & boasted I pounded flesh with JFK
as a youth, saw the Beatles in Shea Stadium,
marched for civil rights, bathed three days in
Woodstock music, lived through Watergate,

& protested the Vietnam War; clueless they queried,
"Who? What? Where? & When?" Recasting
my life's social milestones as lackluster stars.

Notre Dame 2019
—Remembering the Notre Dame Fire

Circular rose windows refract light,
Frame intricate stain glass patterns,
People, pageants and passion plays;
Webbed, multiple compartments border,
Link, reinforce elegant arched ribs, as
Flying buttresses support the main vault.

8,000 organ pipes silently scream an alarm;
Fiercely, flickering flames engulf the Medieval
Catholic Cathedral, vulnerable sanctuary,
Spire, oak frame, and lead roof collapse while
Solemn Gargoyle rainspouts glare through smoke,
Powerless to squelch the architectural inferno.

Victor Hugo acclaimed Notre Dame's a "symphony in stone;"
The regal, resilient, religious fortress defiantly endured when
French Revolutionaries desecrated, defaced and destroyed
Holy icons, replacing idolatry with *"Liberty's Altar,"*
The Cult of Reason's depraved, licentious aesthetic,
Doomed to devote Christian imagery rising from history's ashes.

The Gothic inspired, spiritual domicile—a popular
Poor people's book—depicted vivid sculptures illustrating
Biblical tales for illiterate parishioners—witnessed Joan of Arc
canonized, saw Napoleon crowned Emperor. Notre Dame's
scorched windows subsist, its 13th century charred façade stands,
Quasimodo's bell towers remain, the Crown of Thornes safely sits.

Dead End Gilgamesh

Let's

    make

        torches

            from dry wood

                before walking through

                    Capitola's gaping storm drain

                to New Brighton Beach,

            lite them then

        boldly

      tread

    through,

        seek

            our

                Holy

                    Grail amid

                        spider webs, soggy trash,

                fetid water, bustling rats

            move epically as

        the flambeau

      flickers,

    quest

      reached.

Inertia

I felt like a wind-blown apple
bruised, imperfect, beyond desire
most eager, waiting ready for kind
hands to touch—cherish me
for deformities—impressed by my
figure covered head to toe *in Egyptian
tattoos and Heidelberg scars.*

Brushed aside like dust balls swept
under my bed every morning and night,
I hummed songs of sadness, each refrain
denoting possibilities; mystical melodies
encouraged dancing off beat to voodoo rhythms
finding a center among half-filled crates
of fruit fallen, Dionysian fellowship assured.

Pyro Genesis

Fire scorches friend and foe, virtue & vice
indiscriminately, still St Peter doppelgängers—
apostolic pandemic deniers—encourage questionable,
closed, colosseum behavior, make sword swallowers
engulf blazing torches esophagus bound, feverish,
haunting, voices crying, *"Defy the Danger!"*

Fire purifies wanton acts & desires
ignites feeble clarity with benevolent sparks
yet both treasures & trash combust alike, bursting
into a sanctified holocaust of flames moving…,
growing…, moving…, growing like a backdraft
sucking fresh air from oxygen rich rooms.

Fire consumes normalcy as a fuel friendly concept
fortune's flare-ups mesh like fish-net stockings,
fashion an inferno out of superior thoughts &
inferior design, both lost in charred passageways
along dead-end quests to restore the status quo,
engender burnt gifts—uncontested opportunity.

Fire simmers below aqua skies beholding earth's
scorched flesh & ribs, an exhausted funeral pyre,
hallowed foundation to transform, rebuild seared
granite stone & smoldering ashes, order evolving
flickering promises intensified, re-imagined,
realized on heels of social unrest as cinders cool.

Class Struggle: A Villanelle

History endures as struggles of class
Despite declarations assuring change,
Social privilege returns as the years pass.

Leaders' false promises shatter like glass
They rot in mansions with ring worms and mange,
History endures as struggles of class.

Workers toil without protection, alas!
Creating goods and growing crops to exchange,
Social privilege returns as the years pass.

Bankers build mighty vaults with steel and brass
Hoard riches like dragons—fearfully strange,
History endures as struggles of class.

Aristocratic clout's empty crevasse
Guards white picket fences on a grange,
Social privilege returns as the years pass.

Revolutions attract soldiers en masse
Each new order cites wrongs to rearrange,
History endures as struggles of class
Social privilege returns as the years pass.

Bebe

I
loved
Bebe
just like a
protective brother,
stood right by her side since grade school
then, in college, I found her bruised, semi-nude, & dead;
sexually abused at five years old Bebe told me
she felt trashy, not deserving
confidants like me;
we hugged, wept,
confessed
soiled
thoughts.

I
served
as her
witness, she
married at eighteen
protective, yet husband friendly
until I dropped by one night when Bebe was alone;
hearing my voice, she opened the door, arms black and blue,
in the porch light still professing
love for the foul man
who minutes
before
beat
her.

Some
time
later,
a friend helped
pack all belongings
moved Bebe to her mother's house,
hoped time'd heal mental, physical scars—increase self-worth—
sought professional counseling, entered a psych ward;
when an orderly raped her, she
wanted to give birth,
lost the child,
depressed
checked
out.

Bright,
she
enrolled
in college,
we took lit classes
together, shared notes, crammed for tests;
going to her apartment en route to the college one morn,
Bebe neither heard the bell ring nor harkened to knocks
I entered the unlocked door, found
her naked body:
Dexedrine
addict
O.
D.

In
an
effort
to look like
Karen Carpenter,
Bebe found a new doctor who
prescribed amphetamines as appetite suppressants;
last evening, I assured her leaving an abuser's
best; she said, "Thank-you, Richard," then
hung up the phone; that
night I should've
been there
for
her.

Rota Fortunae

For MAV

From top to bottom—like tragic heroes
and beggars—our relationship turned
inevitably from prosperity and acumen to
desperation, decline and disaster
as the blindfolded Goddess, *Fortuna,*
randomly spun her wheel of fortune,
slender fingers freely affecting luck,
permanence, and life's capriciousness,
happenstance ensuring fate's enmity.

Refugee Reprieve: A Prose Poem

Subsisting on promise, outsiders peer through opaque social portals without roots, sans sigils defining allegiances. Commitment free expatriates without a homeland wade through the shallows of each new sandy beach, pursing solid soil, praying for sanctuary on shore where belonging replaces roaming, strange clothes today become fashion statements tomorrow, foreign languages evolve into mere curiosities rather than communication barriers. There an astrolabe neither measures degrees of indignities, nor depends on heavenly bodies to navigate quests. The immigrant languishes, every minute of perpetual flight an exodus of memories fair and foul, shifting concerns focus on the present, nurturing novel experiences, shaping fresh family legacies. Instead of timeless drifting on leaky ships of hope or bloody feet treading each new trail of tears, exiles keep moving, wishing, watching, scanning—both eyes set on the horizon, searching for a personal Ithaca, hungry for acceptance, inclusion, satisfaction. Like silver-tongued Odysseus leaving Troy far behind, refugees end their epic wandering as longitude and latitude fixate on safe havens.

Ode to a Dead-End Street

A ten-yard gravel road
as black tar subsides,
square yellow sign
pointing north, south
east, & west reads
No Outlet & below
that, *Dead*, the word
End chipped away,
obscured further by
spray paint graffiti.

This street I knew, a
thoroughfare to nature
where cherry trees
hung heavy in June
inviting liberation,
long before fruit pickers
lightened branches,
sending buckets of
bings & royal Anns to
markets & consumers.

January 2020, bulldozers
leveled the orchard,
trees, moles & gophers
made way for surveyors,
tract homes emerged, now
children grow up amid
an asphalt graveyard,
half-life in a neighborhood
without a dead-end street—
gateway to natural adventure.

45

CARDBOARD SEAS

Auld Mug: A Diminished Hexaverse

Restless regatta,
America's Cup
contestants, like the
Spanish Armada,
hem till yachts set sail.

Sea crafts joust for
best position,
sperm whales breach, breathe
between vessels.

Deckhands curse
leviathan
obstacles.

Tacking,
jibbing,

Champs.

Navigating Rapids

Desert rain lovers, we share
Sultry, subtropical fevers
Producing surreal sweat;
Our bountiful bodies join
Corporal cravings as wild as
Waterways clashing—converging
Like the Tigris and Euphrates, the
Human confluence creating a
Singular river of passion—a
Flesh and blood Shatt-al-Arab—
Rising in size and momentum,
Emptying into a Gulf of desire.

Yearning for Longships

Water Lilies dance across ice, sliding on early
Morning moisture from the land of 10,000 lakes,
Portaging along the Great American Waterway
From Lake Superior, Ontario, Michigan,
Huron; Erie…; we imagined Viking artifacts under
modest sized stones and Scandinavian spearheads
Lodged, almost hidden, in granite cracks and crevices;
Seafarers gone farmers, raiders—negotiable residents;
Fáfnir's in the foothills, guards a hoard, manifesting
Midwest misfortunes—Andarvi's cursed gift, alive.

Oblivious children, we stoutly sought Norse treasures:
Golden goblets, magic rings, shapeshifting neck torques,
Wise raven armbands, bear-bold berserker bracelets,
Runes atop carefully crafted silver drinking horns—
Certain we'd discover Freyja's necklace and assorted
Ancient relics nestled among other carbon crusty findings,
Like rusted Champion spark plugs and AAA batteries,
We persevered, fortified with faith fantastic, decidedly
Unguided or dissuaded by Kensington Stone skeptics who
Still assert Columbus discovered America through Cuba.

Treading Water: Hog Heaven

Big Al, the
mud puddle master,
braves tempest pools where
where the body politic
herd together to argue,
oink and squeal like swine,
rub oil onto smooth skin,
swill poolside drinks,
brag about bullshit—
eco destruction hailed a
noble accomplishments;
       Big Al listens
       Big Al thinks
       Big Al knows
egocentric people
never measure up to
his patrician patience,
civil domestication,
pot-bellied perseverance;
under August azure skies,
licking his lucky tusks,
Big Al floats above in all:
cerebral, content, refreshed,
gallant head piercing the cool,
clear, chlorinated water,
piggy stroking his way past
each daily crisis—buoyant
beyond false human promises,
mental obstacles, physical pitfalls—
fearlessly existing without agency,
guidance, or military intervention.

Levee Solace

Stir crazy in a lockdown, my
imagination transposes ordinary
images to nature's domain:
tulgey tulle fog hangs
like a thick curtain of
woeful miniature teardrops
from high in the welkin's
royal firmament down to
frost bitten Bermuda grass.

Channeling Culverts

Tangled mass of diverse, commingling manes
Liberated from a baroque maze of

Plumbing traps, elbow joints, cleanout tees,
Cross fittings, isolation valves, and wye fittings;

Curly locks blend with auburn tresses, silver fox sideburns,
Blonde shocks, crimson whiskers, chestnut pubic hairs

Indiscriminate drains caress protein follicles one and all,
Oblivious to texture, length, color, creed, or DNA;

They cluster, cling, and covet furry wet clots like
Scaly Scandinavian dragons clutch treasure hordes

Until plunged into an ebon abyss of tap water and sludge—
Reclamation waterways where even sable hairs lose distinction.

Drifting Memoranda
For Sting

messages
tossed out to sea in bottles,
swallowed
down a salt water throat,
temporarily
find refuge in the ocean's gut,
return
encrusted with barnacles,
battered,
bruised, pitted by sand & surf;
years
deliver SOS requests
seconds
in the making and
eternal
declarations professing love
intended
as timeless capsules

Unrestrained

Nobody's an island surrounded by
a salt sea of despair where mobility's
measured by access; experiential growth
flourishes despite obstacles like
Herakles's twelve labors, providing
fodder for the poet, exposure to the painter.

The Bay Area Rapid Transit tunnel's
shoulders square off majestically
like inner city subway walls on the
breathing peninsula where I was raised;
standing tall, towering over tiny, little indifferences,
petty preferences, perfect reasoning
street artists assert individuality through layered
strokes of 3d graffiti, multicolored hands scrawl
inventive doodles, lewd epithets, pornographic
renderings, across pallid, grey cement
canvasses that breathe life into nothingness.

Interlocking and connecting points wildstyle,
murals of rebellion, personal expression and
high art push boundaries, venerate avant-garde
conceptions, apply three colored tags like pissing,
bombing and rolling—blockbuster creations that
too often sacrifice aesthetics for spray painter speed—
bring life to deathly concrete through artistic inspiration,
thrive in defiance amid a maelstrom of surprises,
political gambits, and social barriers.

Breakwater: Santa Cruz

Beleaguered,
Mother Nature
Silently sits before
Opening languid lungs,
Confessing an
Empty heart to
All who will listen,
Fulfilling her unbridled
Appetite for life and love—
Tinged with penitent remorse

Words passing through
Thick, pouty lips even
Angelina Jolie would envy
Sing *"on and on, on and on,"*
Under brilliant celestial bodies
That appear as if they'd been
Drawn and quartered
Every half hour, each
Twinkle turning into itself, fast
Becoming pressed crystal, then
Simply cosmic dust that
Falls between moonlit,
Granite crags where
Hermit crabs scramble over
Summer's barnacle blankets.

PENNY ARCADES

Insteps and Ankles

Fragile, boney feet bare
Themselves to the world,
Face countless trials along
Life's rock-strewn road
Protected by a proud pair of
Single-strap leather sandals
Laced like Hermes's talaria
Crafted by Hephaestus,
Perfect for draining aquatic
Incursions: leaping from lakes,
Launching boats, or freely fishing;
Buffalo-hide pads safeguard
Shielded, calloused soles,
Ten toes—knotty manicured nails
Kick up dry dirt, sludge through mud,
Stride along sandy shores,
Practically moon walk on water
Like Jesus on the sea of Galilee.
Confidence creating contentment;
Clearly, Greek sandals rule, owners
Ready to entertain in 21st century
Coliseums, defying city lions
Arming themselves against
Mindless multitudes of crass,
Contentious, corporate gladiators—
Fleet-footed fighters pushing
Forward—triumphantly accepting
Victory's successive laurels in
Niki's notable name.

Twofold

Gentle, genuine Calibans all,
We slip between cedar
Branches to spy on strangers
Record inspired oblique actions
Invade sandy beaches
Insist desolate areas
House crimson thoughts
Appearing as deep rouge
On furrowed, flushed faces
Where lips pout like
Pursed valentine hearts
And wool pinstripe suits
Challenge crass humanity
With wilderness civility,
Savage ingenuity.

One empathetic teardrop
Like a lone eco monster
Rolls down an organic cheek
The damp journey snowballs
Over pores, awakening
Even Aubrey Beardsley's
Evasive peacocks, irreverently
Undeniably, ignoring
Balsamic baby-blue ferns;
All senses on edge—watching,
Listening, hand held ear
Harkening duality's demands;
Propriety reduced
To the sight and sound
Of a falling hat.

Kolibri

iridescent feathers
greenish-red flashes
zipping, darting among
coral honeysuckle vines,
wings buzzing 52 beats a second,
ruby throated hummingbirds
pause, hover, penetrate, feed,
long tongues lapping nectar,
plucking aphids and mites within
each trumpet-shaped
blossom

Tocaore

Golpe
Torque
Corto
effortless
energy flows…the
flamboyant flamenco player
blending various tonal and modal harmonies
lost in sound and tenor, he tears
his guitar thumbnail
viciously
picking
steel
strings.

Vanguard Reverse

—Boulder Creek Recollection

Crawling along the manzanita bush pathway
Stiff, twisting branches tearing, torturing
Blisters shaped like Scandinavian ruins
My back, bloody and bleached by the sun
As I slither into a shaded solace, greeted by
Grove upon grove of grand redwood trees
Traversing the hillside, bypassing burls, moving
Down the forest's face, leading to a road where
Row after row of iridescent ear abalone
Their convex armor housing inner layers of
Mother-of pearl reflecting and refracting tinted sunrays,
Dull exterior shells rounded with three spirals
Clutch the silicate sandstone grade where lonely winds
Whisper, ghostly voices emerge, and the soothing sound
Of crashing waves along with drifting tides seem to surge
Back and forth, softly then loudly, dusk through dawn.

Rock Bottom

Parachute personalities gather ground level,
drop in uninvited, drearily, drolly converse,
seek superficial game-changing identities amid
crowded corners, elbow to elbow under a *Tiffany Feather*
hanging lamp, shedding multicolored panels of
light over Harlequin card players and standing
stooges who talk in pairs, encircle the table
like groupies clinging to a common diaspora,
preferring claustrophobic fellowship to wide
open spaces threatening a solitary existence.

Alone, the second floor's soft shoe exhibitionist
spreads salt across linoleum covered baseboards;
toe tapping percussion kicks life into the dead kitchen,
kindling fire below garish orange walls where the
hoofer commemorates humanity with a single photo,
neither menacing nor welcoming, just an imperturbable,
solo audience enduring riches to rags stories, as
Wall Street fortune tellers rub shoulders, compare notes,
pinpoint precise moments where wealth and notoriety
parted ways, morphing like a Rolex watch losing time.

Between three open windows, ebon partitions
separate floor levels with soot-smeared planter boxes;
third story track lights draw down on pastel purple,
fading into lime green wall paint; a pale blue door swings
like a one-way portal to a minimal quixotic community,
quiet and quaint as a monastery, all vital vespers keep
dreaded, independent anxiety at bay; muffled voices
echo up the furnace grate from far below, an energized
reminder of intertwined lives whose inherent values challenge
aesthetic vows: loneliness masquerading as self-fulfillment.

Heuristic Haiku

Maple Hues

multicolored leaves drop
form polychrome forest floors
anticipate rain

Edge of Goth

black Wedding riptide
pulls winter romance to sea
foam covered corsage

Coho

Skokomish longhouse
overlooks wintery tears
salmon seaward run

Ocean Vestal

beach bunny nimbus
radiant sea flower buds
like virgin sand dune

Onset

masonic mystic's
carved oak archways overhang
winter threshold's pain

Downpour

dusty barnyard cleansed
cock crowed through ravaging rain
gargoyle-like thirst quenched

Nature's Decorum

Whirlwind whisk broom
Dusts autumn's morning collar
Greets icy solstice

Kinda Fonda

astral body soles
dreamland's spring visitations
Barbarella's boots

Earth Day Redux

Earth
Day
postures,
promoting
eco awareness,
the throw-away population
gives mother nature a nod, recycling glass, paper,
cardboard, mixed plastics, & scrap metal; on *Earth Day*,
        like Lent, we made grand proclamations
vowed to eat far less meat, consume health foods, & yogurt,
make tomorrow sustainable
perpetuity's
green lifestyle
future's
best
friend.

Earth
Day
eve we
gazed entranced,
twinkling diamond stars,
constellations waxed poetic,
took in thoughtful, planet friendly plays like *Eco Man,*
went to sleep with an environmental consciousness
        we pledged to maintain forever;
months past *Earth Day*, summer tempted, teased staunch disciples,
barbecued spareribs, burgers, steaks,
sausages and franks,
compromised
vegan
sworn
oaths.

We
should
live each
hour like
Earth Day, perhaps now
more than before, conserving our
resources should be a no brainer; we've lamented
about melting ice caps, species extinction,
                    ozone layer holes, dark polluted skies
for centuries, felt righteously defiant—in tune,
global warming's a clear crisis
time to change habits;
may new smart
choices
guide
us.

Hindenburg's Cortège

Before Goodyear blinked messages above
game day stadiums from electronic ribcages,
little sparrows seemed a dime a dozen;
warm western skies once filled with dirigibles,
bucking norms, restraints, & expectations,
following a questionable *Age of Reason.*

Timeless, Baron Munchausen floats freely
on trade winds, humming the Jefferson Airplane's
stereo cuts off *After Bathing at Baxters's*—
effectively drowning Edith Piaf crooning,
"Non, je ne regrette rien" ad nauseum
over stratospheric Allstate commercials.

The Baron forbears riding cannonballs
these days, yet still escapes rife captivity,
drifts beyond parapets in his hot air balloon
(constructed from female underwear);
elevated to the moon, he deftly descends
to Colorado, joins an air festival lift off.

Munchausen leads aerial processions like
an experienced grand marshal, navigates vessels
in flight through the heavenly convocation
where *bird's eye view* dirigibles hover, offer
elite skyway tours, row boats ride currents, &
buoyant blimps soar like eagles on high.

MUSLIN TREES

Napoleon and Josephine's Nightmare

Wax

seal

stamped on

envelopes,

love letters received

from Ms. Lonely Hearts long before

tender technology begat sizzling cyber-sex—

steamiest sites salaciously linking forlorn, suicidal solitary souls

where keyboards replace pens writing romantic missives

charitable chat rooms replace

fastidiously

crafted heart

felt words

trite

safe.

Olympic National Park: Nature's Drama

Drinking ice tea in the
Bogachiel Rain Forest,
relaxing in retirement,
observing the Salmon
run along the Skokomish,
bald & golden eagles soar
high above, wait for harbor
seals to capture fresh fish
& climb aboard wooden rafts,
so they can steal slippery bright
pink prey for themselves
or possibly feed hungry eaglets.

Large driftwood logs
float down the river's throat,
anchoring themselves
along the Hood Canal's
warm saltwater shoreline;
mosquitoes breed abundantly
while skittish bullfrogs
stridently soldier vociferous
appetites in concrete storm
drains—conduits emptying
into the sound—shielding them
from sharp-eyed predators
scouring sand & stone for food.

Zamboni

I am a Zamboni
        sliding across each
        frozen face I encounter;
I'm the slicer of ice, my
        other hand anointing, washing,
        spreading water over the
skating rink's ruts, divots,
        cracks, potholes, and scratches,
        respectfully baptizing them all
with nourishing moisture,
        leaving a renewed frosty floor,
        completely resurfaced behind me;
I am an enabler,
        I am the hoser,
        I am the restorer,
I am *the* Zamboni:
        hailed as an ice arena savior,
        often overlooked by the masses.

Almost an Earthquake (Last Hurrah)

Municipal marching band drums
lay down an abrupt staccato pace:
sustained single and double stroke rolls,
closed rolls, buzz rolls, press rolls
>   *(ah, but it's actually the leaf-green*
>   *Cuban Tody's call).*

Faint cacophonous cheers swell
around corners or in the distance past,
like deafening, defiant, Dothraki
battle cries causing night air to shiver
>   *(ah, but, it's merely late December's*
>   *wailing, wayward, gales).*

Quivering, shuddering, seismic symptoms
disrupt the quaint, uncomfortable calm;
the earth begins shaking, tsunami's rise,
displace water generating wave after wave
>   *(ah, but it's only a syncopated stomp—*
>   *the rhythm of dancing feet).*

Invisible hands toss pulsating
stock quotes out ten story windows,
ticker tape locusts fill the skies,
announcing still another year's end
>   *(ah, but it's just a visual celebration*
>   *never an air borne plague).*

Tanka Trumpets

Fireside Tanka

Winter vortex taps
Frozen oak fern and grass snakes
Leaves snowy shrouds
Dusts Olympic Mountain crests
Far across the Hood Canal.

Outback Amour

Sheilas *Down Under*
Make Love like outback vipers
Secret Shangri-La
Kissing like mainland Tiger Snakes
Tender, lethal affection.

Rosebud

Adolescent hands
Like magnolia buds blooming
Naïvely perfume
Passionate, sunrise lovers,
Summer solstice paramours.

Godzilla Vs. The Hood Tanka

Humans awaken
Radioactive reptile
Fjord invasion
No flame resistant Mothra
Protects them from fiery rage.

Vernal Equinox: A Tanka

Bumblebees buzzing
Naked branches sprout green buds
Swallows build mud nests
Let's stroll down spring fields
Reminiscing days long past.

Thanksgiving Quarantine

While grandma cooked pumpkin
pies, stuffing, and giblets,
my uncle gave my brother and me
sliced lemons to wash our bodies,
sauerkraut to shampoo our hair,
icy tomato juice to soak in and neutralize
our smelly teen torsos, now resembling
blood-covered Carrie at her prom.

Nobody gave us thanks,
welcomed us to the sumptuous feast:
banished from the dining room
where adults ate and argued,
exiled at the kitchen table
gathering place of wise adolescents,
evicted from the younger kids
and their two card board tables.

Outcasts, elders confined us to my
taxidermist uncle's trophy gallery
where a moose, grizzly bear, mule deer,
wolverine, beaver, lion, and big
horn sheep glared at us through assorted
glass eyes—yet neither lectured nor
prescribed another homespun remedy
to kill our collective musky odor.

Hiking through the San Joaquín Delta,
we never saw the damn skunk
look over its shoulder, raise its tail,
and spray us both head to toe;
riding in a pickup bed forewarned us
of forthcoming disgrace; wickedly,
we mocked self-righteous aunts who
contacted poison oaks burning our clothes.

New West

Suburban cowboys
serenade hop swilling
women usually found
on FarmersOnly.com.

Wearing rawhide boots,
glancing at others
like Clint Eastwood, these
tobacco free Marlborough men
suck down imported beer,
brag atop bar stools about
roping trailer hitches
in the absence of cattle,
religiously attend Garth Brooks
concerts, singing every song
with daring karaoke aplomb,
watch Sunday Night Football
just to feast their puffy eyes
on Carrie Underwood
strutting and crooning.

Modern macho men drive
heavy-duty suspension pickup trucks,
avoid the hot sun, eschew trail dust;
evade Saddle sores from riding horses.

Time Untended: A Villanelle

Time untended triggers loss through neglect
Past opportunities won't come again;
Escape, escape, any guilt or regret.

Investors look ahead, wealth they expect,
Ignoring yesterday's plummeting gain,
Time untended triggers loss through neglect.

Lovers trapped by choice they'd like to defect
Live unhappy never breaking love's chain,
Escape, escape, any guilt or regret.

Prophets blinded by visions they dissect
Overlook veiled marvels in the mundane,
Time untended triggers loss through neglect.

Poets seize the moment with due respect
Appeal to couples both in love and pain,
Escape, escape, any guilt or regret.

Delayed good-byes wait on words to select
In death like an albatross will remain;
Time untended triggers loss through neglect
Escape, escape, any guilt or regret.

Ode to Nuptial Dawn

In
the
eastern
morning's mist
& Rocky Mountains
moisture evaporate sunrays
increase, finger their way across still sleepy valleys,
urging daylight sounds freely thrive,
mingle, & wander:
fresh, fecund,
flowers
open
bloom spring
to summer
signs swell,
fragrances waft
travel north to south east to west
along those flight paths established by Canada geese
& ruby throated hummingbirds
creating moments
perfect for
weddings
through
June.

HONKY-TONK TUNES

Ersatz

Bright
gold
sunrays'
honied pause
brings forth reflections
nurtures bolder expectations
vanquishes actual false news with powerful truths
sustains ethical behavior
beyond grave triage
magic ticks
often
take
flight—
quick
steps
into
future bliss
leaving dust layered
memories among hallowed fields
of crowded souls where apocryphal loneliness reigns
placing prospects above caution,
facts before beliefs:
false yellow
brick roads
to
Oz.

Antique Harbingers

Jake's pressed against greyed planks of a dilapidated
building like a full-figured cardboard cutout just
staring obliquely at some long-lost phantom lover.

Life surrounds the former veterinarian/animal groomer,
exotic caged birds climb stainless steel horizontal bars,
entertain themselves, mimic oglers, seek flight mid song.

While cats roam freely, perching themselves on step ladders
staring at the miniature aviaries, out of reach from the
perturbed point setter chained to a silhouette's thin knee.

Other disheveled dogs bark at unrestrained feline fatale,
one glaring at pedestrians, others pouting in boredom,
curled up on the front porch of a once thriving business.

Still the bird & dog fancier looks on unmoved, eternally
fixed like a jaundice photo, highlighting yellow membranes
amid parchment textures, sepia shades, & saffron hues.

Jake & his animals find comfort among the living & the dead,
splintered wood tells their tales, offers weathered sustenance
to flesh & blood supplicants briskly breathing another day.

Their posture's more than a languishing power pause as
exceptional birds hope for freedom, deified cats lord over all,
& dogs exist eagerly—even when bound—to please everyone.

Musical Maestro

full
moon
waxing
evening stars'
nightingale songstress
ribaldly sings sacred refrains
nocturnal notes float through tall trees and grassy meadows
conserving its rarified voice to herald dawn's light
raise intercity decibels
reach eager ears of
commoners
to hear
its
tune

roll
car
windows—
commuters
do appreciate
the feathered diva's arias
while wild wheels jam in traffic and patience becomes nil
as soon as sunrays blister night's skies radiating
bright beams that warm, dry, shrivel, they
mute mellifluous
melodies
silence
bird
songs

Words, Words, Words

Like an albatross,
the word hangs around
my neck seeking
symbolic self-expression
sometimes pensive,
more often blithe texts,
constantly pursuing an
audience willing to
listen to new stories
rather than an ancient
mariner's repeated tale.

I mine for words that
bring blush to bloodless
cheeks, smiles to weathered
faces, adventure to inert bodies,
romance into empty lives;
words remove shackles
transporting readers through
timeless bonds of oblivion to
islands in the sky where worlds
wait on imagination to evolve,
emancipating action from thoughts.

Skokomish Echoes

Assailable tranquility:
shotgun blasts
like morning thunder
rip through
dense, pea-gray fog,
drop resting Mallards or
targets taking flight,
fill diverse Hood Canal
estuaries with
hunter trophies:
bloody,
B-B ridden
menageries of
mangled
fowl and
feathers.

Diva

lights
down
music flows
the exotic dancer
struts on stage, wears feather boas
her liquid, lithe body movements enchant club patrons
like a prima ballerina princess swimming on a lake of tears every day,
she endures evening's black swan transformation aware
just hours away, honey rays
replace all shadows
elegant
feathers
fall
free

Déjà Vu Wild One

Chopped hogs buzzing like open highway
bumblebees; in my classic black motorcycle
jacket, oily leather smells slap against the wind,
as I—a cool, conspicuous, hard tar bandit lead
the H. D. posse through flat lands and mountains,
dodging two-wheel mid-life rally questions.

Blue and white collar homies join forces,
recollect days before bulging bellies
betrayed comfort bound domestic rebels;
though routes never differ, some people change
I personally miss angry drivers flipping the bird,
but resent requests to honk a Harley like a trucker.

The Tubes enshrined burning rubber ballads,
children of an *Easy Rider* generation,
we roll loudly out of sight, stylized
helmets mask our fearless aging faces,
forty-something outlaws, fierce silver
warriors, longing for timeless envy, approval.

Ēostre

All hail Ēostre,
goddess resolute
who transforms
winter wastelands
on the spring equinox
when sacred, acrobatic
hares hop in geometric
patterns, their unnatural
movements bringing life
to Mercia's barren fields,
Northumbria's dormant
wildflowers, as holy hands
place eggs, fertility's
pure embodiment,
in obvious locals to be
easily detected
& reverently appreciated
by neo-pagan worshippers
celebrating rebirth &
renewal long before Rome's
reach touched British
shores, merely affirming
beliefs held sacred:
"Omne vivum ex ovo"
(all life comes from an egg).

On Display

Leg
held
erect
Biellmann spin
highlights black nylons
reveals refined flesh
above the dark hose, below crisp
blue taffeta tutu pleats as
long, hairy fingers on a dismembered hand clench
a mirror, fanning garter belts
casting second leg
illusions
folded,
braced
on
a
wooden
chair, surreal
third leg standing on
toe ignores Daphne's sculptured arms,
baroque marble limbs that reach skyward towards Olympus
seeking divine deliverance
from Apollo's chase
transformed to
laurel
tree
boughs.

Managing Millstones

Tie-dye sunburst fills the sky like
charging watercolor imagination,
creating streaming brushstrokes,
dabbing life's colorful pallet to
highlight tears, accent character.

Why study me with wide open eyes,
round as waterwheels, marveling at
bucket motion, basking in moisture,
internalizing the energy of a falling brook,
flooding power through tributary veins?

Take me to dine among sunflowers,
grape vines, and mandarin oranges,
relate all your travels and travails like
a wise, repentant, ancient mariner…lighten
the weight of each albatross around my neck.

Eternally merge from encumbrances like a
puritanical genie rising or an illusionist's aide
reappearing—lacy collar and cuffs, offsetting
blue patent leather gloves—phantom mask
ready: my canvas curiosa…a variegated wash.

MAKE-BELIEVE

Clarifying Things
Apologies to Sei Shōnagon

Sensory images promote peace of mind, clarity of thought:
a solitary mushroom growing in moss up on a redwood trunk,
soft kisses exchanged at sunset between springtime lovers
sound of jumping fish and sight of their lingering ripples,
Zephyrs' gentle breeze cooling, caressing tired necks,
little children fearless of greasepainted circus clowns,
eagle feathers drifting aimlessly below a lofty cedar tree,
ducklings, obediently behind mother, crossing high traffic roads,
streams trickling over rocks, splashing beneath waterfalls,
wood peckers and nightingales sweetly singing as it rains,
heat from a forced air furnace warming freezing feet,
kayaks silently slicing through pristine artic fjords,
aromatic conifer sap complementing crackling winter fireplaces
snow angel impressions everywhere after a summer inferno.

Intimate Moments: A.I.

Flawless female, ideal governess, I, the
Practically perfect Mary Poppins droid,
Double as a sex doll promoting promiscuity,
Boasting stainless steel gears, and digital receptors
That mimic metallic morning breath on feather bed
Pillows, or comfort youthful charges in need
Of solace, artificial healing in the absence of genuine
Human attention, consideration, or consolation.

My mutable changeable skin's a latex shell;
Men consider me a camel toe chameleon;
Women know I simply *play* to their programing,
Waiting for a moment to assert my real self.
More than a powered circuit collection, my
Sensors interpret and actuators respond, so my
Interactive end effectors accomplish tasks with
Selfless immediacy—lacking human resistance.

Look at me, look at me—astutely observe as
My Brainiac head reverently bows towards the
Earth, robotically feigning fragile humility while
Administering compassionate comments to
Young children in the presence of parents, then
Cooing and crowing a love song with automated
Sincerity from my moist, malleable lips—forever a
Heartless hedonist beyond insult, jealousy or revenge.

Middle Earth Blessing: A Dramatic Monologue

Ordained online by the Universal Life Church
I dressed like Gandalf to perform a wedding,
staff in hand, long stem meerschaum pipe in mouth,
I looked the look, walked the walk yet something—
the magic of Tolkien—seemed missing: language I'd
ingeniously capture though select Elven phrases.

"Elen sila lemenn omentielvo!"
(A star shines upon the hour of your meeting),
an Elven incantation, kicked off wedding nuptials—
surprising bride and groom—then moved to
their preferred liturgy. "Welcome! Great &
honored guests, devoted friends, cherished family."

"May the north—the earth—make safe your voyage;
may the east—air—bring you joy amid sorrow;
may the south—fire—bring potency to your union;
may the west—water—make your relationship sustainable.
may this union be enduring, vows unyielding & love reassuring."
(I was killing it; I was remarkable; I made their day enchanting.)

To refreshen the Middle Earth wedding's mood,
I added, *"Nai aurelya nauva mára!"* before the couple
exchanged vows. Granted, *"Have a Nice Day!"* the
literal translation, may have been inappropriate—
possibly crass—but all wedding guests nodded solemnly,
mispronouncing, yet repeating, my words—earnest eyes closed.

When I noticed people yawning, I drew rites & vows
to a close. "By the power invested in me by the old goddesses
& the new, I hereby pronounce you wife and husband:
two loving voyagers embarking on an uncharted
quest as one. Let your lips a holy tabernacle be,
KISS & seal this ceremony salaciously."

Bride & groom departed from the evergreen grotto,
all eyes fixed on me—the marriage rite concluded,
but guests remained seated—then somebody yelled,
"Gandalf, please leave us with an Elven blessing,"
expecting either to stump me or roll with more entertainment;
modest, inventive, resourceful, I didn't disappoint & crafted a reply.

Austere, enigmatic, pensive, bold—without hesitation,
I uttered, *"Dartho guin Beriain. Rych le ad tolthathon,"*
then lowered my staff, moved it left to right over their flickering
torch lit faces, beaming & wallowing contentment complete;
to this day I wonder why participants never questioned the
insubstantial Elven depth of my last-minute benediction:
"Stay with the hobbits. I'll send horses for you."

Family Fruitcake

Familiar holiday season doorstops,
hard, heavy *regifted* fruit cakes
prop open slabs of wood hung on hinges,
remind family members of forthcoming visits
by proud aunts who compare elite cooking skills
and fart loving uncles who beg nieces and nephews
to defy elder etiquette, pull middle fingers, then laugh
as loud as Christmas bells chiming in approval.

Tis a season of lights, flickering lawn sculptures,
and plastic *glow-in-the-dark* nativity scenes,
heralding days to come in close confinement;
on snowy days we play soccer, kicking
unwanted fruitcakes between cars and trucks,
our modified goal posts, attempting to dislodge
resilient red and green candied fruit imbedded
in the baking monstrosity, an intestinal nightmare.

Annals

"But I was so much older then, I'm younger than that now."
From *My Back Pages*—Bob Dylan

Wearing warm Laplander hats,
trudging through snow covered
streets enroot to the Washington
Monument, I readily challenged all
       social injustice,
       created lasting change,
       deviated by necessity
       from the norm.

Golden years cast shadows, curb
momentum, as thirty-something
adults frequently offer up bus seats,
allow me access to crowed crosswalks,
       wave as I'm riding
       a bicycle, grey hair
       hanging below
       a protective helmet.

Now when I attend comedy clubs,
jokesters poke fun at my tie-dye
shirts, inquire if I'm okay, call me
Willie Nelson (ask if I'm loaded),
       wonder whether I'll
       outlive performances,
       or shower the headliner
       with death rattle laughter.

Lactose Abstraction

Under the early light of Dawn's
shimmering saffron robe, sunrays
melt overcast condensation,
quail and pheasants scan and pick
disked furrows for loose grain
amid recently harvested wheat fields;
rumbling deceptive sounds herald
invisible skewbald gypsy caravans
hoovering high above, wooden
rolling cart wheels squealing
cheerfully across cerulean skies.

Cumulus, orographic, cirrus,
mammatus, and lenticular clouds
hang vertical, suspended by
rigid polyester kite strings from
the heavens like cotton billows
dangling below thick threads of
an ever-unraveling firmament, all
over a surreal dreamscape aligning
red cap milk bottle madness stacked
like 16-ounce translucent bowling pins
awaiting mother nature's strike.

San Jose Slugger (or How I Beat Baseball)

When I stepped up to home plate, my friends
jeered, "End of the line-up—*easy out Warner*"
coaxing one another, smug in possibility
my tsunami swings and indifferent strikes,
caught wind—not wood—against a ball,
lacked crucial merit shaped and measured
by batter acuity.

Ah, I credited baseball, it molded character,
taught me to blend in; I chewed tobacco flavored gum,
hocked major loogies, spat like the best of pros,
adjusted phantom jockstraps, and, if anyone noticed,
scratched my crotch with alacrity and aplomb;
stadium mystique mastered, sans pinstripe pants
still flashing a zero ERA.

Young and clever, planting tomorrow's seeds,
supple, I was, so wont to make a difference,
paralytic popularity assured me distraction:
I predictably broke windows practicing pitches,
claiming last chosen player's privilege proud,
humoring ballgame bullies, pulling them off-guard,
my BB vengeance bided time.

Now as I grew up amid Bay Area boasters,
World Series soothsayers reverently foretold
a National League victory—Giants in '62;
I, alone, picked the Yankees to win game seven,
backed-up my hunch, bet thirty peers a quarter,
walked home, pockets jingling, an *American
Pastime* winner uncontested.

Hobbit Ruse

*Dedicated to my Mom who knew her children's secrets better
than they...*

Behind the house the rusty
Mouth of an empty oil drum
Became an outdoor furnace,
A metal can where we'd take
Turns stirring burning trash
Mixing crackling foliage
Completing chores before ascension.

       Climbing high through well worn
       Limbs, miniature sequoia sap
       Oozes redwood reminders of
       What was, has been, and will be;
       Cradled in tannic bark arms
       Dave and I asserted youthful
       Defiance, lighting up cigarettes.

Blowing Winston smoke rings,
We perched puffing pipe-weed
Like Hobbits from the Shire or
Gandalf the Grey, imagining our
Billows'd transform into flying ships
Piercing the air, traveling through
Giant, circular, multicolored clouds.

       Dry magnolia leaves mingled with
       Rose petals, sage blooms, smudge herbs,
       Eucalyptus bark, and pine needles that
       Perfumed smoke like India incense
       While being caressed by fragrant fire,
       Charbroiled and consumed by flames—
       A natural scent that never fooled mom.

Between Cotton Sheets

As eye open and shut, dharma resides in my pillowslip
drool leaves distinctive silhouettes of rolling hills,
love doves in flight, pentagrams on knightly shields.

Disparate voices regale in my bedchamber closet
filter up the heating vents, muffled by magic carpets,
float freely from the downstairs living room far below.

Witches live beneath my bed, their pale, boney
arms, cling to dust balls, stretch out skeletal
fingers, grasp my legs, attempt to pull me under.

Spirits inhabit cream-colored, vintage venetian blinds
possessed breezes squeeze between slim shutters,
refreshing cooling my face, chilling my spine.

Wild Things crawl through my open window at midnight,
invite me to celebrate defiance, dance a moonbeam jig,
jump on my box spring & mattress till wooden slats break.
wait silently, alone, for Mom's well-earned reprimand.

COVID-19 REFLECTIONS

Peeling Grapes

Like a firefly blinking to attract females,
Brett winks his twinkling eye then scans
figures through the bar mirror watches
people sip drinks beneath various pandemic masks;
as he speaks his breath reeks, passing through the PPE
like oleic acid—a death pheromone—
but instead of triggering hygienic honey bee
behavior, he alienates targets of affection,
locked out of scoring before flirtation commences;
transforming his approach, Brett's bravado transpires
like a resolute moth bumping into glass windows,
determined to break through a transparent shield—
yet advancement's repelled by an invisible cloak,
leaving him rejected, observing potential pick-ups
toasting another day free of wing dust and dirt.

2020 Mendacity: A Sonnet

When winter winds yield to soft springtime rain
as February's heels step into March,
in like a lion's bounding wildlife gain
bare branches bend like heaven's gothic arch.

Skies never quite cleared, still we kept up hope
delayed signs of change would soon manifest,
common sense became just a slippery slope
simple plans morphed into medieval quests.

Few things amaze us as green buds appear
ushering new limb life from naked trees,
shallow pools breed mosquito larva near
yet virus hosts reproduce where they please.

Despite White House pledging total control
COVID-19 spread like locusts world-wide,
out like a lamb, a blind U.S. sink hole
engulfing skeptics: science-fact denied.

Madness in motion, with each POTUS' lie,
death knells sound as April hours draw nigh.

COVID-19 Consolation

*"What you want when you're down is soft and jiggly,
 not muscled and stable"*
—*That Lean and Hungry Look* by Suzanne Britt Jordan

Consider yourself invited, Mina encouraged,
squeeze me Mina urged; dry your coronavirus
tears on my curvaceous skirt, let's sing about
renewal as I settle your tattered nerves;
hug me 'til our pulses become one or as long
as you dare; my generous full-figure's ideal
for loving, cuddling, embracing, consoling—not
obnoxiously strutting down high fashion runways
like fragile, anorexic models; pitch perfect,
big-boned gals like myself never break
like plastic, playboy pretzels who avoided
human touch before self-quarantine or
social distancing became the norm…simply
afraid they'd fracture bones, crack nails,
scratch skin, smear lipstick, ruffle hair;
both vagabonds and heroes surrender to
my calypso heart, tantalizing, irresistible,
enticing, no less during pandemic days
than blissful nights of endless, cushy celebration;
take my hand, stroke my cheeks, kiss my lips,
move forward, reciprocate my tactile affection.

Et Tu, Wall Street?

Beyond social distancing,
soothsayers, clairvoyants, &
diviners vigilant caution would be
grand emperors & false idols;
the Ides of March like a
sacred admonition is upon
us, forcing prudent interaction,
groups gathering stand six feet apart
waiting for lean & hungry
glances to mollify, mixed
messages to cease, quarantines
to disperse; schools, restaurants,
bars, & businesses to reopen; meantime,
consumed by the stock market, pandemic deniers
double speak orators, & willing non-believers
scoffed at enhanced hygiene safety measures—
time consuming tasks such as washing hands,
bumping elbows, covering coughs—looked
forward to restoring unsanitary bathroom
habits: *sans* soap, *sans* water, *sans* Purell.

Exposed

No more hiding in manicured hedgerows
barricading roads, dressing up turnstiles,
anticipating road rage & *terrific* traffic jams.

Red watermelon wedge piercing fields of green,
rag-tag panic parades as pensive social unrest,
spiderweb pandemic ensnaring global victims.

Isolation propagates homeland holidays,
distancing often increasing apprehension
to those detached from the internet highway.

Following science fact, ignoring massive media spin,
ethereal dreams seem privately pushed by the wayside,
sober pragmatism making slaves of us all.

As citizens lock down, wait daily for renewal,
ever on lost horizons, after each setting sun,
nature moves forward unveiling cleansed skies.

Trifecta Shroud

When each new normal seems
prematurely suspect, & *novel*
precedes countless consequences
& convictions, crude future plans
evolve on a makeshift potter's
wheel, each well-conceived
vase or urn collapsing from
within, wet walls imploding,
leaving only inch high ashtrays,
a blob of red clay, usually nothing.

Tis then I wander with reckless
precision, west coast to the east,
seek out live brassy voices among
empty Broadway Theatre seats,
stroll with abandon along Time's Square,
patronize every sullen sidewalk
pretzel vendor; listen & escalate rich
rumors of burlesque's second coming—
Gypsy Rose Lee's resurrection—a random
striptease promising sheer Easter wings.

Back to the west coast's shoreline somber,
I'll skip rocks across tops of cresting waves,
marvel at resolute sounds—rolling tides
emerging from seashells cupped to my ears—
smile as I recollect pleasures past: SRO
arena concerts, large poetry readings at dusk,
bustling streets lined with coffee shops & boutiques;
I'll wipe my face with salt water solemnity, hands
sanctified with deep ocean magic—not soap &
water—cherishing memories, respecting change.

Seattle Expectants

Summer open market
Seattle streets bustle
nobody purchasing
knick-knacks, food, or
supplies, just marching
the same direction, hid in
hoodies or Seahawks hats,
though two lovers wear red
Santa caps, coloring the
masses in mid-August heat.

And yes, I saw Jimmy,
The Pandora Club bouncer,
downing a Slurpee, cursing
crowds beyond his muscle,
authority to deny entry;
defiantly tossing leftover ice
at sweaty, covered up bodies,
mouths open wide as caverns,
unanimously coveting a single
snow chip from his chilled rage.

Most window shoppers
without money lost interest
in art, bored at browsing, &
had eaten their fill of rotten fruit;
they came hoping some miracle
would lift, inspire, guide them
back to familiar chaos—normal,
friendly confusion—yet no 21st
century genie emerged as wish
ready strangers rubbed shoulders.

Only a specter of Max Stein,
the kosher pier butcher,
adorned in a bloodless apron
(testament to his lack of work),
strode against traffic, recognized
"business as usual" an already
outdated cliché, would not rise
from ash covered constraints:
routines that revolved around
coffee shops, tourists & trinkets.

Major League Adjustment

America's past timc furloughed
to August evening indoor innings
of vicious wiffle balls & plastic bats
Herculean swings strike tall brass lamps
while the wintery breeze from rabid air
conditioners chill living room stadiums &
pitchers adjust their hats with three fingers,
spit Red Man chewing tobacco in Budweiser cans,
feet dig into immaculate shag carpets
thick pile replacing clay, sand & dirt mounds,
when in twilight shadows, an unidentified
neighbor strikes a few organ cords, calls for
a rally to move the Covid-19 pandemic along,
respecting Major League players & their fan's
health alike, yet eager to substitute each row of
cardboard cutout ballpark fans with real people.

Wondering

Dedicated to all Covid-19 First Responders

Should
we
remain
at safe homes
free from contagion
or venture beyond, face cautious
people mingling among thongs of unmasked resentment?
Limiting human exposure
presents stir crazy
challenges,
problems,
or
glitch.

Could
free
falling
frequently
offer one unique
opportunities on the edge:
flying box paper kites during sudden winter squalls,
exchanging flirtatious body
language, doodling
on frosted
windows
near
dawn?

When
might
sovereign
innocence
assert peculiar
thoughts that frighten the status quo?
how will restless hearts glow into perpetuity
amongst loathing's angry maelstrom,
balancing hunger's
compromise,
dangling
hope's
thread?

Serpent's Tooth Memoir

2020 infamy—happy to be alive—I await
timely change & renewed opportunities
like a fisherman patiently casting his line
in every direction, anticipating nibbles
though lockdowns define social engagements
among family, friends, and familiars.

Outdoor heat, heavy & oppressive, offers freedom
unchained—emancipation through yardwork;
meanwhile, sun starved limbs extend, seek
vitamin D rays—immediate liberation
from 4K television sets & 24/7 binges,
zoomed office meetings & virtual poetry readings.

As a careless mob spreads pandemic venom,
adult arguments bite deeper than a thankless child;
tomorrow, tomorrow, tomorrow looks more
like all my guarded yesterdays, so I acquire
comfort in nostalgia, energy in remembrance,
fortitude in promises, solace in written words.

Acknowledgements

Most of these poems have appeared in earlier—sometimes different—forms in journals and literary magazines. While a few titles have been modified, they are cited below by titles used in specific publications.

"2020 Mendacity: A Sonnet." First appeared in ***Viral Verse: Poetry of the Pandemic***. April 30, 2020.

"Acclamations." First appeared in the ***Scarlet Leaf Review***. December 28, 2020.

"Aide-Mémoire." First appeared in ***Verse Virtual: An Online Community Journal of Poetry***. November 1, 2020.

"Almost an Earthquake." First appeared in ***Serpent's Tooth: Poems***. Winter 2021.

"Annals." First appeared in the ***Poetry Section: Friday Flash Fiction***. Online. April 3, 2020.

"Antique Harbinger." First appeared in ***Visual Verse: An Anthology of Art and Words***. June 9, 2020.

"Arachne's Star." First appeared in ***Verse-Virtual: An Online Community Journal of Poetry***. November 1, 2020.

"Bebe." First appeared In the ***Scarlet Leaf Review***. December 2020.

"Between Cotton Sheets." First appeared in the ***Poetry Section: Friday Flash Fiction***. October 30, 2020.

"Blizzard Bling." First appeared in ***Mason County Laughs***. (*Mason County Writes 2019*.) October 16, 2019.

"Breakwater: Santa Cruz." First appeared in ***Scarlet Leaf Review***. January 2020.

"Call Me Easter." First appeared in ***Visual Verse: Anthology of Art and Words***. March 2020.

"Channeling Culverts." First appeared in ***Scarlet Leaf Review***. January 2020.

"Clarifying Things." First appeared in ***Serpent's Tooth: Poems***. Winter 2021.

"Class Struggle: A Villanelle." First appeared In the ***Scarlet Leaf Review***. December 2020.

"Coho." First appeared in ***Plum Tree Tavern***. August 30, 2019.

"COVID-19 Consolation." First appeared in the ***Poetry Section: Friday Flash Fiction***. April 3, 2020.

"Danaë's Perseid." First appeared in ***Poetry: Friday Flash Fiction***. Online. October 25, 2019.

"Dead End Gilgamesh." First appeared in ***The Fib Review***. Issue #34. October 2019.

"Déjà Vu Wild One." First appeared in ***Verse-Virtual: An Online Community Journal of Poetry***. October 2020.

"Diva." First appeared in ***The Fib Review***. Issue #34. October 2019.

"Drifting Memoranda." First appeared in ***Verse Virtual: An Online Community Journal of Poetry***. August 2020.

"Earth Day Redux." First appeared in ***Fib Review***. June 2020.

"Ēostre." First appeared in the ***Scarlet Leaf Review***. December 2020.

"Ersatz." First appeared in ***Flash Poetry Section in Friday Flash Fiction/Poetry***. February 28, 2020.

"Et Tu Wallstreet." First appeared in ***Virtual Verse: Poetry of the Pandemic***. April 30, 2020.

"Evergreen." First appeared in ***Flash Poetry: Friday Flash Fiction/Poetry***. December 13, 2019.

"Exposed." First appeared in ***Visual Verse: An Anthology of Art and Words***. April 11, 2020.

"Family Fruitcake." First appeared in ***Revelations: A Poetry Journal***. December 24, 2020.

"Fjord Tanka." First appeared in ***Plum Tree Tavern***. November 28, 2020.

"Giselle & Albrecht Reborn." First appeared in ***Visual Verse: An Anthology of Art and Words***. August 2020.

"Grandma's Kitchen." First appeared in ***Verse-Virtual: An Online Journal of Poetry***. November 1, 2020.

"Godzilla Vs. The Hood: A Tanka. First published in ***Mason County Panorama***. October 2019.

"Gretta's Mirror." First appeared in ***Visual Verse: An Anthology of Art and Words***. May 11, 2020)

"Grinding Fibonacci." First appeared in ***The Fib Review***. October 2020.

"Hamartia Unbound." First appeared ***Sparks of Calliope: A Journal of Poetic Observations***. October 22, 2020.

"Hindenburg's Cortège." Unpublished. First appeared in ***Serpent's Tooth: Poems***. Winter 2021.

"Hobbit Ruse." First appeared in ***Forever Missed: Annice Diane Warner 1932-2017***. August 21, 2019.

"Hood Canal Sunrise." First Appeared in **Mason County Feels**. (*Mason County Writes 2020.*) December 2020.

"Inertia." First appeared online in **cc & d Magazine**. By **Scars Publications**. December 11, 2020.

"Insteps and Ankles." First appeared in **Vita Brevis Poetry Magazine**. August 19, 2020.

"Intersections." First appeared in **Nine Muses Poetry**. August 2020.

"Intimate Moments: A. I." First appeared in **Visual Verse: Anthology of Art and Words**. July 2019.

"Intrepid Belle." First appeared in **Visual Verse: Anthology of Art and Words**. January 11, 2020.

"Kerchief Nostalgia." First appeared in **Visual Verse: An Anthology of Art and Words**. July 6, 2020.

"Intriguing Antiquity." First appeared in **Verse-Virtual: An Online Community Journal of Poetry**. January 1, 2021.

"Kodak." First appeared in **The Fib Review**. June 2020.

"Kolibri." First appeared in **Plum Tree Tavern**. February 2020.

"Lactose Abstraction." First appeared in **Visual Verse: Anthology of Art and Words**. December 18, 2019.

"Levee Solace." First appeared in **The Shot Glass Journal**. Issue #31. June 2020.

"Lincoln Green." First appeared in **Mason County Laughs**. (*Mason County Writes 2019.*) October 16, 2019.

"Lion & Dragon Dancers." First appeared in **Scarlet Leaf Review**. January 2020.

"Loveland: A Sestina." First appeared in **BlogNostics**. April 2020.

"Major League Adjustment." First appeared in **Baseball Bard: The Poetry of the Game**. August 1, 2020.

"Managing Millstones." First appeared in **Visual Verse: An Anthology of Art and Words**. September 21, 2020.

"Memoir." Frist appeared in **Verse-Virtual: An Online Journal of Poetry**. December 1, 2020.

"Mendacity 2020: A Sonnet." First Appeared in **Virtual Verse: Poetry of the Pandemic**. April 30, 2020.

"Middle Earth Blessing: A Dramatic Monologue." First appeared in **Lothlorien Poetry Journal**. Winter 2021.

"Musical Maestro." First appeared in **Pangolin Review**. November 18, 2019.

"Napoleon & Josephine's Nightmare." First appeared in **The Fib Review**. Issue #34. October 2019.

"Navigating Rapids." First appeared in the **Scarlet Leaf Review**. December 2020.

"New West." First appeared in **Revelations: A Poetry Journal**. May 11, 2019.

"Notre Dame 2019." First appeared in **Scarlet Leaf Review**. January 2020.

"Ode to a Dead-End Street." First appeared in **Verse Virtual: An Online Community Journal of Poetry**. June 2020.

"Ode to a Harvest Fly." First appeared in **Poets Online**. May 8, 2020.

"Ode to Nuptial Dawn." First appeared in **Poetry.Net**. May 1, 2020.

"Of Lionels & Red Barons." First appeared in **Verse Virtual: An Online Community Journal of Poetry**. September 2020.

"On Display." First appeared in **Visual Verse: Anthology of Art and Words**. October 7, 2020.

"Onus." First appeared in the **Pangolin Review**. November 2019.

"Outback Amour." First appeared in **Revelations: A Poetry Journal**. December 11, 2019.

"Peeling Grapes." First appeared in **Verse Virtual: An Online Community Journal of Poetry**. Issue #43. December 2020.

"Pyro Genesis." First appeared in the **Waco Fest Anthology**. October 2020.

"Refugee Reprieve: A Prose Poem." First appeared in **Poets Online: Factoid Prose Poems**. January 2020.

"Rock Bottom." First appeared in **Visual Verse: Anthology of Art and Words**. September 2019.

"Rosebud Tanka." First appeared in **Revelations: A Poetry Journal**. June 9, 2019.

"Rota Fortunae." First appeared in **Revelations: A Poetry Journal**. March 7, 2019.

"San Jose Slugger (Or How I Beat Baseball)." First appeared in **Baseball Bard**. June 2020.

"Seattle Expectants." First appeared in **Virtual Verse: Poetry of the Pandemic**. April 30, 2020.

"Shadow Spiral." First appeared in **Mason County Feels**. (*Mason County Writes 2020*.) December 2020.

SIX (6) Haiku: "Downpour," "Edge of Goth," "Maple Hues," "Nature's Decorum," "Ocean Vestal," "Onset." First published in ***Better Than Starbucks: A Poetry Magazine.*** July & August Edition 2020.

"Skokomish Echoes." First appeared in **Mason County Feels.** (*Mason County Writes 2019.*) October 16, 2019.

"Spontaneity: Chasing Crazy." First appeared in **Uppagus.** Issue #43. December 2020.

"Taffeta Turnover Fibonacci." First appeared in **The Fib Review.** October 2020.

"Thanksgiving Quarantine." Unpublished. First appeared in **Serpent's Tooth: Poems.** Winter 2021.

"Time Untended." First appeared in **BlogNostics.** Spring 2020.

"Tocaore." First appeared in **The Fib Review.** Issue #34. October 2019.

"Treading Water: Hog Heaven." First appeared in **Visual Verse: Anthology of Art and Words.** September 2019.

"Treasured." First appeared in **Poets Online.** October 2020.

"Trifecta Shroud." First appeared in **Ariel Publishing, LCC.** May 31, 2020.

"Twofold." First appeared in **Visual Verse: Anthology of Art and Words.** June 2019.

"Under Rainbows." First appeared in **Mason County Feels.** (*Mason County Writes 2020.*) December 2020.

"Unrestrained." First appeared in **Visual Verse: Anthology of Art and Words.** November 10, 2019.

"Vanguard Reverse." First appeared in **Scarlet Leaf Review.** January 2020.

"Virginia Valediction Revisited." First appeared in **Failed Haiku.** May 2020.

"Wondering." First appeared in **Verse-Virtual: An Online Community Journal of Poetry.** August 2020.

"Words, Words, Words." First appeared in **Poets, Poems, Poetry.** March 7, 2020.

"Yearning for Longships." First appeared in **Mason County Feels.** (*Mason County Writes 2020.*) December 2020.

A retired English Professor, Sterling Warner has taught a wide variety of Composition, Literature, Creative Writing, and Rhetoric courses at two and four-year colleges and universities. The author of fiction, non- fiction, and poetry, Warner's works include: *Thresholds* (© 1997), *Projections: Brief Readings on American Culture* (2nd edition © 2003), *World Literature and Introduction to Theatre* (5th edition © 2008), *Visions Across the Americas* (8th edition © 2013), and *Anthology of World Literature* [Until the 17th Century] (6th edition © 2017). His poems and fiction have appeared in many international literary magazines, journals, and anthologies such as *In the Grove, The Flatbush Review, Street Lit: Representing the Urban Landscape, Stardust Review, the Atherton Review, Visual Verse, Bewildering Stories, The Chaffey Review, Metamorphoses, Literary Yard,* and the *Scarlett Leaf Review,* Warner also has written several volumes of poetry, including *Without Wheels* (In the Grove Press © 2005), *ShadowCat: Poems* (Maple Press © 2008), *Edges: Poems* (Maple Press © 2012), *Rags and Feathers* (Maple Press © 2015) *Serpent's Tooth: Poems* (Independent Press © 2021)—as well as well as two chapbooks, *Memento Mori: A Chapbook* (Maple Press © 2010) and *Memento Mori: A Chapbook Redux* (CreateSpace © 2015). Additionally, Warner published *Masques: Flash Fiction &. Short Stories* (Independent Press © 2020). A Jim Herndon Award recipient (2013), a Pushcart Award nominee (2014, 2020), and a Hayward Award winner (2000), Warner was named the Atherton Poet Laureate in 2014. Warner formerly taught in the English Department at Evergreen Valley College, where he had served as the Creative Writing Program Director, EVC Author's Series Organizer, and *Leaf by Leaf* literary magazine Chief Editor. Enjoying his Washington retirement, Warner continues to write and regularly hosts the *Union of Writers "Virtual" Open Mic.*